SO YOU WANT TO SET THE PACE

So You Want to Set the Pace

INVESTING YOUR LIFE IN OTHERS

CHUCK KLEIN

Tyndale House
Publishers, Inc.
Wheaton, Illinois

Unless otherwise noted, Scripture references are from *The Living Bible* © 1971, Tyndale House Publishers. Other Scriptures are from the *New American Standard Bible* (NASB), © Lockman Foundation, 1960, 1962, 1963, 1968, 1971.

Fourth printing, August 1986
Library of Congress Catalog Card Number 80-50903
ISBN 0-8423-6083-2

Printed in the United States of America

Contents

Introduction: Do You Want To Set The Pace?

Jesus Christ doesn't call us to mediocrity. That's just plain contrary to his nature. Jesus calls men and women to significance—to be his special communicators in a world that is screaming for reality. *Jesus has plans for his disciples!*

In 2 Corinthians 5:20, the Apostle Paul hangs the tag of significance on each one of us. It's a tag that gives each of us an identity, a purpose, a reason to exist in this world as one of God's children. The tag reads: *Christ's Ambassador–his authorized courier.* The job description: lead people to a personal relationship with the One who created them. Our authority: all the authority of Jesus Christ himself.

Contrary to what some folks think, being Christ's ambassador is not an option; it's a command. But if you have come to know anything at all about Jesus Christ, you know that he never gives a command without also providing all the resources to do the job, which really makes the job much more conceivable. Christ requires just two things from you, his ambassador: your *attention* and your *availability*. Anything beyond that the Lord can't use. It's just wasted energy.

So why not ask yourself a couple of questions? Do you feel like a significant person? Do you consider yourself someone important? A giant void can exist in our lives when we fail to see ourselves the way God really sees us, as the most important person for his most important job—*reproducing new disciples.* That's a bigger purpose than anyone's void, and that's the purpose to which he has called you.

How to Use So You Want to Set the Pace

So You Want to Set the Pace is designed for study groups and for personal study and growth. *So You Want to Set the Pace* is created especially for Christians who want to learn the basics of investing their lives in others.

So You Want to Set the Pace is written in progressive studies. This means that the chapters build upon each other, and it is best to study them in succession. The questions are designed to help you discover truth on your own. The illustrations will help you visualize what is being taught.

To use this book you will need a Bible and a pen or pencil. If you are using *So You Want to Set the Pace* as a part of a group, it will be very helpful to prepare for your discussion by filling in the answers to the questions in advance of your meeting.

At the end of each chapter there are *Action* assignments and personal study assignments designed to help you apply and internalize the truth being taught. Between group meetings, set aside time each day to study these portions of Scripture and talk to God. Purchase a notebook that you can use to keep a running log of the things God teaches you in your action assignments and your personal study. Discuss the things you are learning with the other members of your group.

1 Who Are You?

Before we talk about your ministry, maybe we should first talk about who you are. It may make all the difference in the world. This little illustration will help us get started.

Let's suppose you were 5′2″ tall—not typical basketball team material. One day the coach of your local college basketball team approaches you and asks you to be the center on his team. You would wonder how this guy ever became a basketball coach. One good look at yourself next to a tape measure would convince you that you are *not* a basketball center.

But let's suppose that something very unusual starts happening to you. You start growing dramatically, and you keep growing. Before you know it you have grown to nearly seven feet tall, and you aren't an uncoordinated clod, either. This same coach then comes to you and challenges you again, "I want you as the center on my basketball team."

Now, intellectually you know there is something different about you. Your clothing bill tells you that. But you have a slight problem. You don't really feel like a seven-footer. You still *feel* and *think* like a five-footer. You are used to looking up, not down. You are used to getting out of other people's way, not other people getting out of your way. Your *identity* (the way you see yourself and think about yourself) has not yet caught up with who you really are, and until it does you will never be able to perform as a basketball center, even though you have the ability to do so. *You have an identity crisis.*

The Christian Identity Crisis

This is a funny little story, isn't it? You might even think it's kind of silly. After all, no one changes that much in that short a time.

However, in the spiritual world I know a lot of folks who have been dramatically changed but still see themselves as they used to be, not as new creations. They see themselves as strugglers, not as powerful victors. They think it is normal to lead a fruitless life, not to be fruitful. *These people are Christians who suffer from a bad case of identity crisis.*

The Truth about You

The *key* to living the Christian life and ministering to others is *knowing who you really are.* In 2 Corinthians 5:17-20 Paul describes who we are and what we are because of our relationship with Jesus Christ. Read this passage carefully and see if you can discern the *two facts* of who you are in Jesus Christ.

1. ______________________________

2. ______________________________

What does Paul say happened to the old things of our lives? (See verse 17.) ______________________________

____

____

Paul establishes two facts of our identity. One, as Christians we are *new creations in Christ.* And second, we are now *God's ambassadors*—his special, personal representatives.

WHO ARE YOU?

Do you feel like a new creation in Jesus Christ? Well, maybe you do and maybe you don't. Paul is not talking about how we feel; rather he is talking about who we really are if we have entrusted our lives to Jesus Christ. Feelings are always a result of knowledge.

Take a look at each of these Scripture verses and explain what each says.

Romans 6:4, 5. ______________________________

____

____

Ephesians 2:10. ______________________________

____

____

In Ephesians 2:1-6, what tense (past, present, or future) does Paul use to describe the old life? ____________________

In your opinion, what is the significance of this tense?

____

____

The problem that many of us have as Christians is that we place our *identification* in what we were, not in what we have really become in Christ. We think that we are just the same old person who happens to have eternal life. Consequently we tend to live like the old person—sin is normal and power to live a new life is abnormal. In a sense we have the same problem as a seven-foot basketball player who thinks and acts like he is still five feet tall.

But Paul tells us that the power that once controlled our lives, the old sinful nature (our old identity), was actually *dethroned* and *shattered* when we trusted Jesus Christ to come into our lives. Now we no longer have to obey the desires of the flesh. We can focus on our new identity in Christ and trust the Holy Spirit to fill us and give us his power.

When I see myself as a new creation in Christ I begin to expect something much different as a normal way of life. My desire to grow in Christ dramatically changes *because of who I am and what I know God wants to do in me.*

Created for a Purpose

Now if you are a new creation in Christ, what *have you been created to do?* Let's look at another illustration. This one will require a good imagination.

Suppose you owned a beautiful, thoroughbred racing horse, one that could talk, like Mr. Ed (I told you this would take imagination). Your horse is bred and raised to win races. Now one day a rabbit approaches your horse out on the race track and suggests that they take off together and live the leisured life of a rabbit. They would eat carrots, take in some rabbit games, and raid gardens. It would sure beat working hard at the track every day.

After some intense persuasion your horse packs his bag and takes off with his new friend to begin his life of leisure. But it doesn't take long for him to realize that he is a very bored, unfulfilled horse. For him there is no satisfaction in hopping and eating carrots all day. He is a horse, his identity lies in being a horse, and meaning for him exists in running races at the track. He is going to be very unfulfilled until he can do what he was created to do.

WHO ARE YOU?

Another offbeat story? Yes, but there is a point here. *You will never find meaning in life if you are not doing what you were created to do.*

Let's apply this to our spiritual lives. If we see ourselves as fundamentally the old person we were before Christ came into our lives, then we will try to find meaning in life in the ways that the flesh finds meaning. According to Galatians 5:19-21, where does Paul say that the flesh looks for meaning and fulfillment? ______________________________

____

____

____

(Envy, anger, and strife are some of the fleshly emotions of someone who feels he has been deprived of something he needs for meaning and satisfaction.)

Where Is Your Meaning?

As we have discovered, you are not fundamentally a fleshly person. You are fundamentally a new creation in Jesus Christ and you will never find satisfaction and meaning in the desires of the flesh. Your flesh thinks you will, but that's not who you really are.

Where will you find meaning and purpose in life? If you have learned anything at all about God, you know that the instructions in his Word are designed to give you the ultimate in satisfaction and purpose. Getting into the Word, communicating with God, allowing the Holy Spirit to fill you and lead you are the sources and resources God has provided for your fulfillment.

In Ephesians 2:10, Paul describes a very special plan God uses to give us a sense of significance and purpose in our lives. In this Scripture verse Paul tells us that we are *God's workmanship.* What do you think it means to be God's workmanship?

____

____

According to this verse, what has God created you to do?

____

When was it determined that you would do these things?

____

Do you think you will find purpose in life doing anything else?

__________ Why?______________________

____

What are some good works you believe God has given you the opportunity to do this past week? ____

Did these good works give you a sense of purpose? ____
Why? ____

What are some good works you think God has in store for you this coming week? ____

You Are an Ambassador

In 1 Peter 2:9, Peter first tells us who we are (our identity), and then he explains what we do (our purpose and meaning).

According to this verse, who are we? ____

Because of who we are, what are we supposed to do? ____

Has it ever occurred to you that you will find real meaning in life as you share Christ with others? Don't we usually look at a ministry of sharing our faith as a very unnatural activity, but do it because God instructed us to? Listen carefully to Peter. *You are a chosen* [*person*] . . . *God's own possession, so that you may proclaim the* [*praises*] *of him who called you* (NASB).

When we realize who we are, then sharing Christ becomes a natural part of what we do.

Let's wrap things up by looking back at our original Scripture passage in this study, 2 Corinthians 5:17-20. We are a *new creation in Christ*. Now we can naturally pursue what he created us to do.

According to verses 18-20, what are we to do because of who we are? ____

What do you think it means to be an ambassador for Jesus Christ? What does an ambassador do? ____

So you see, meaning for you is walking with Christ and introducing others to him. Nothing else can really fulfill you, because trying to do or be anything else is not being consistent with who you really are.

Putting It All Together

Have you discovered that you have not fully realized who you are in Christ? ____________________

Explain what new truth you have learned. ____________________

____

____

____

In what way do Christians have the same problem that the basketball player had? How could a Christian overcome this problem? ____________________

____

____

____

THANKS, COACH!
I ALWAYS SAID YOU HAD WHAT IT TAKES!
MVP

Does knowing who you are in Christ make a difference in how you feel about yourself? Explain your answer.

____

____

____

____

Why would knowing your true identity help you as you think about developing your ministry to others? ____________________

____

____

____

____

"The most *significant* thing I have learned in this study is:

____

____

____________________."

For a more in-depth study of our identification in Christ and how to live a supernatural life, see *So You Want to Get into the Race*, chapters 3-6 (Wheaton, IL: Tyndale House Publishers).

My Action This Week—Prayer

Pascal, the French philosopher said, "There is a God-shaped vacuum in the heart of every man which only God can fill through his Son, Jesus Christ." Have you considered the *vacuums* in the hearts of people around you who do not know Christ? These people are looking for meaning and purpose for their lives, but they are looking in all the wrong places.

What can you do to help them find Christ? The place to begin is on your knees, *talking to God.* This week your assignment will be to make a list of at least five people whom you desire to see receive Christ. Begin praying for these people daily, asking God's Spirit to reveal to them their need and to give them a hunger to know him.

At your next group meeting be prepared to share some of your prayer concerns.

My Personal Study This Week

- 1 Timothy 2:1-4; John 14:13, 14; Luke 18:1-5; Matthew 18:19; Romans 8:26. What do these Scripture verses teach you about praying for others? What promises can you claim?
- Philippians 3:3-11. List the good things in Paul's life that could have given him some meaning and purpose. Why did Paul consider these things rubbish? Where did Paul find his meaning and purpose? (List everything.) What does this teach you?
- Romans 12:1, 2; Colossians 3:16; 2 Timothy 3:15-17; Joshua 1:7, 8. How should you nurture the new you? What role does God's Word play in building you up? Why is God's Word absolutely essential to help you live as a new creation in Christ?

Concepts in this chapter have been inspired by David Needham's book *Birthright* (Portland, OR: Multnomah Press, 1979).

2

But Can I Do It?

We have discovered that having a ministry in the lives of others is a very natural extension of who we are in Jesus Christ. In this study we are going to discuss the foundation, the starting point, so to speak, of our ministry to others. Can you have a significant ministry? You sure can, if you build on the right foundation.

A Question of Priority

Let's suppose that you planted some fruit trees in your backyard, watered them regularly, and gave them plenty of fertilizer. It wouldn't take long before they would be bearing fruit. But what if you stopped fertilizing them and cut off their water? How much fruit would they produce then? The answer is obvious. Probably none. There are certain necessities that are basic to growth and to life. Without them, life is impossible.

In your spiritual life the same principle is true. You are not going to be a fruitful Christian just because of knowledge, or training, or hard work, or even natural ability. *Fruit in our Christian life is totally dependent on our source of life.*

In Romans 7:4, how does Paul describe what has happened to us in order that we might bear fruit? ____________________

____

____

____

BUT CAN I DO IT?

It is a biblical fact that as a Christian you are spiritually joined to Jesus Christ, and this relationship is going to bear fruit. In John 15, Jesus talks about your responsibility in fruit bearing. You are no doubt familiar with it. Read John 15:1-8 and explain what you see as the main message of this Scripture verse.

What does it tell you about Jesus Christ?

What does it tell you about yourself?

What does it tell you about the lordship of Jesus Christ? (Lordship means Christ's absolute leadership of your life and your response to his leadership.)

Use some words that you think would describe what it means to abide in Christ.

Do you think a person could bear fruit and not abide in Christ? Why?

Do you think a person could abide in Christ and not bear fruit? Why?

The specific fruit that Jesus refers to in John 15 is the fruit of our prayers (vv. 7, 16), joy (v. 11), love for others (v. 12), and the result of our ministry to others (v. 16). Fruit also includes the fruit of the Spirit in Galatians 5:22, 23.

A Relational Life-style

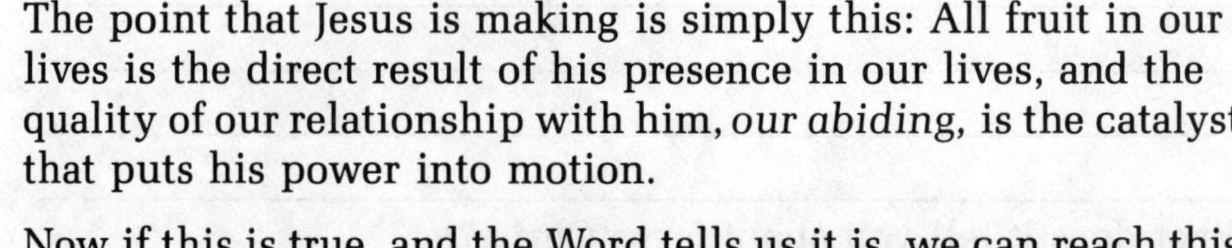

The point that Jesus is making is simply this: All fruit in our lives is the direct result of his presence in our lives, and the quality of our relationship with him, *our abiding*, is the catalyst that puts his power into motion.

Now if this is true, and the Word tells us it is, we can reach this conclusion: *A healthy, growing relationship with Christ is going to produce a healthy, fruitful ministry,* not because of your ability or training, but because Christ is allowed to work in and through you. Ministry is not an issue of trying but an issue of trusting.

On the other hand, *if our relationship with Christ is hurting,* then for us a personal ministry will seem like climbing Mt. Everest—one big, hard job. We will try to accomplish the job by our own ability, we will perform for God, and we could expect some predictable results—frustration, guilt, fear, and a good case of spiritual burnout.

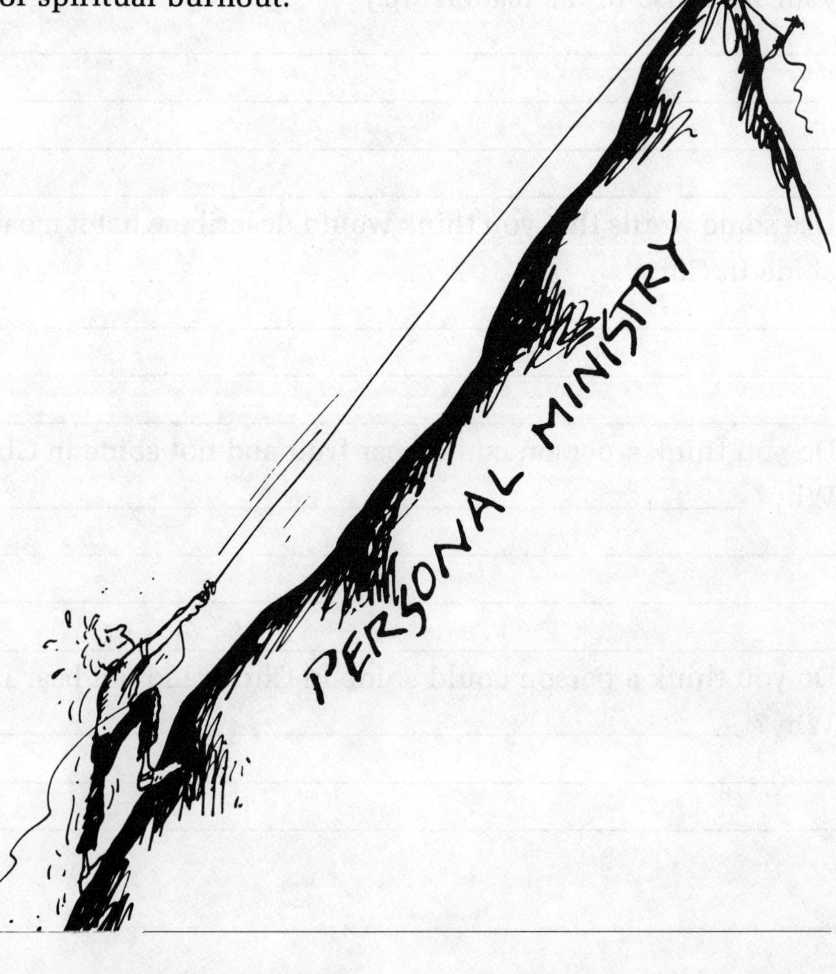

BUT CAN I DO IT?

How would you describe a healthy and growing relationship with Christ? What would it look like? List some characteristics.

How would you describe an unhealthy relationship with Christ? What would be some characteristics?

Getting Healthy

According to John 15:2, what does God do in our lives in order that we might become more spiritually healthy and productive in fruit bearing?

What do you think it means to be *pruned* or *trimmed* by God?

Pruning in this passage refers to a *cleaning* that God does in each of our lives. He *disciplines* us, he *transforms our minds* by his Word (v. 3 and Romans 12:1, 2), he graciously *removes* those things from our lives that draw our faith away from Christ and hinder our fruit bearing.

Christians who rebel against God's pruning and who will not trust Christ with their lives may be taken out of Christian service by God (vv. 2, 6).
What pruning has God done in your life recently?

Conditions for Feeding Sheep

In John 21:15-17, Jesus gives us more insight into this whole area of our relationship with him and the effect it has on our ministry.

In this Scripture verse Jesus asks Peter the same specific question three times. Each time Peter gives the same answer, and then Jesus gives him a command. What is Jesus' question and what is his command?

What do you think Jesus meant by *feed (or shepherd) my sheep?*

Why do you think it is significant that Jesus asked Peter if he loved him? Why do you think he asked him three times?

From what you see in this verse what would you describe as very important in our own lives if we are going to care for and minister to others?

Peter learned over the years that love for Christ will always manifest itself in service to others, because in reality we are serving Christ—the one we have come to love. Listen to what Peter said in his latter days.
"Feed the flock of God; care for it willingly, not grudgingly . . . but because you are eager to serve the Lord" (1 Peter 5:2). Service is demonstrating love for Christ.

Love You? Well . . . uh . . .

I have often wondered what Jesus would have said if Peter would have answered something like this: "Well, Jesus, I think I love you, but you know we haven't been spending much time together, and I've been real busy with a lot of other things, and . . ." Is this how you would have answered Jesus?

I think Jesus would have said something like this: "*Peter, I want you to feed my sheep. But first let's spend some good personal time together. Perhaps we need to straighten a few things out. I love you. I want you to love me. After all, I'm the one you are going to be proclaiming.*"

BUT CAN I DO IT?

Jesus never says that we have to reach a certain plateau of spiritual maturity before we can minister to others. In fact, you will grow spiritually as you do share your faith and help others grow (John 4:31-34). What Jesus is telling us is that our ministry and our lives are sustained by our growing love relationship with him. That's what John 15 and 21 are all about.

Let's think about your life for a moment. How would you describe your relationship with Christ right now?

____

____

____

Could you say to Jesus right now that you love him? ________

If your answer is *yes*, why do you love him? ________________

____

____

____

Love is not just a feeling, but it is also *doing* something for the one we love. How could you demonstrate your love for Christ today? ________________________________

____

____

____

Putting It All Together

To wrap up our study, let's turn back to John 15. In your own words, explain what Jesus says in verse 16. ______________________________

What do you think Jesus means when he says, "I have chosen you"? ______________________________

Do you believe God has chosen you to bear fruit in a ministry to others? ______________________________

If the key to bearing fruit is the vitality of your relationship with Christ, then what areas of your Christian walk do you think need special attention and development—maybe some pruning? What could you do to grow in these areas? Pray about these questions and then commit yourself to some plans for development. (You will really have to think about this.)

PERSONAL DEVELOPMENT WORK SHEET

Areas of Growth	*Plans for Development*

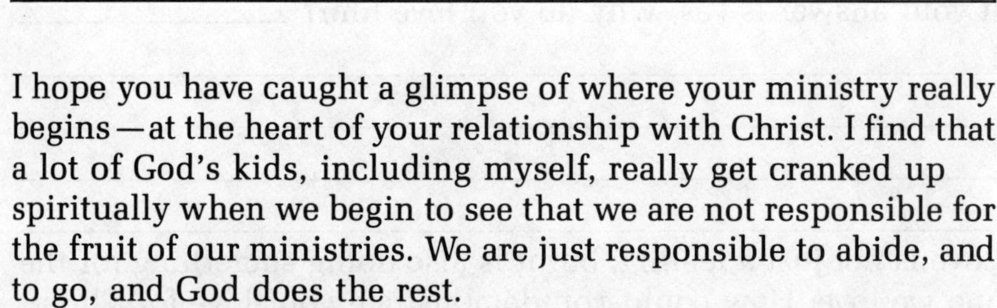

I hope you have caught a glimpse of where your ministry really begins—at the heart of your relationship with Christ. I find that a lot of God's kids, including myself, really get cranked up spiritually when we begin to see that we are not responsible for the fruit of our ministries. We are just responsible to abide, and to go, and God does the rest.

Successful ministry is abiding in Christ and then being available to people. Your ministry is all around you!

BUT CAN I DO IT?

- John 17:20-26. What does this passage teach you about Christ's concern and love for you? What truth in this Scripture passage arouses your love for him?
- Jeremiah 1:4-19. When did God choose Jeremiah for his ministry? What was Jeremiah's excuse? What was God's reply? What promise did God give to Jeremiah? What did he ask Jeremiah to do? List all the truths and principles from this passage that you can apply to your life and ministry.
- Isaiah 40:29-31; Luke 12:11, 12; Psalm 37:1-7; Ephesians 3:20, 21. In answering the question, "Can I do it?" what do each of these verses tell you? Why can you do it?

My Personal Study This Week

3

Your Ministry at Home

In Mark chapter 5 we read the story of a man who was dramatically changed by Jesus Christ. In verse 18, as Jesus prepared to move on in his ministry travels, the man begged Jesus to take him along. But Jesus instructed him otherwise. What did Jesus tell him? See verses 19 and 20. ____________

____

____

As a Christian, where does your ministry really begin? Out in the limelight, or back at home in the presence of your family? In this study we are going to talk about your relationships around your home and how God can use your *right attitudes* to open up opportunities to minister to your family.

The Family Plan

Your relationship with your family is second only to your relationship with Jesus Christ. God has placed you in your family (Psalm 139:13-16) and designed your family specifically for your growth and development. So it would be wise to understand exactly how God wants your family to function.

Let's look first at the responsibility of those who are in authority in your family. From each of these verses, describe the responsibility of your mother and father. Describe the positive results of their role in your life.

1 Timothy 3:4, 5 ______________________

Proverbs 13:24 ______________________

Proverbs 22:6 ______________________

Proverbs 29:15, 17 ______________________

Deuteronomy 32:45, 46 ______________________

What does Paul tell us about the role of our parents in Ephesians 6:4? ______________________

Let's just suppose that you have a parent who is not always loving and does tend to provoke you to anger. Does this mean that God cannot use this parent in your growth and development? Why? ______________________

Perfection is something we all like, especially when it comes to our parents. But God has a remarkable way of using imperfect people in each of our lives just as he uses us in others people's lives. God uses all parents, no matter how well they measure up to the standards of his Word. He often uses them apart from their own knowledge.

In God's Word the spiritual condition of our parents is never mentioned as a factor for obeying their wishes. Think about it.

Character Building

The Lord is not interested in how mighty we are in ability, or ministry skills, or knowledge. Rather, he wants us to be mighty in character, and it is in your home where character is born. How you respond to your parents, brothers, and sisters determines how well your character will be built.
Listed in the margin are some of the character traits that God wants to build into our lives.

attentiveness
dependability
discernment
integrity
generosity
humility
kindness
love
obedience
perseverance
respectfulness
teachability
unselfishness
forgiving attitude

According to each of these Scripture verses, how does God want you to *respond* toward other members of your family? What *character* trait would each response help build?

Proverbs 13:1 ______________________________

____

____

Ephesians 4:29-32 ______________________________

____

____

Ephesians 6:1-3 ______________________________

____

____

What promise can you claim? ______________________________

____

I REALLY DON'T
THINK YOU
SHOULD
DO THAT.

Philippians 2:14, 15 ____________________

1 Timothy 4:12 ____________________

1 Peter 3:8-12 ____________________

When you feel you have been treated unjustly at home, what attitude really finds favor with God? Why? See 1 Peter 2:18-21.

Of the Scripture you have just studied, which verse do you feel you especially need to apply to your home life? Why?

If you do not learn to relate and build relationships at home, it will be difficult for you to build relationships outside of your home. That is why every difficult situation you face in your family is your opportunity to learn how to successfully deal with that problem.

Your home is God's primary classroom in preparing you for your life and ministry.

Focusing on the Right Things

We have discovered that God uses our homes to build godly character. An important quality of godly character is to concern oneself with the needs of others, not just with one's own needs. Without God's character we tend to be just the opposite. We selfishly focus on our own needs, and we complain about those around us who fail to meet our needs. We criticize them for their lack of character. Is it any wonder we have so many problems at home?

YOUR MINISTRY AT HOME

Explain what Paul says about this in Philippians 2:3-7.

Opportunities to minister at home will open up all around you as you begin to focus on the personal needs of each of your family members. What are their needs? How can you demonstrate a special concern and interest in their needs? Use the following work sheet to think this through.

FAMILY NEEDS WORK SHEET

Family member	*Special needs they have*	*How will I demonstrate my desire to help meet this person's need this week?*

Some Questions to Think About

Suppose you had a ministry activity coming up and your parents were also planning a family activity and wanted you to be involved. Which activity should you attend? Why?

What spiritual truth have you learned recently that you would want your family to learn also?

How should you demonstrate this truth at home? What changes may have to take place in your behavior? ________________

____

____

____

Is there someone in your family who has not trusted his or her life to Christ? Read 1 Peter 3:15 and list the practical guidelines for sharing Christ with this person.

____

____

____

____

My Action This Week—Building a Relationship

As we wrap up our study, think about this question: With which member of your family do you especially need to build a closer relationship? ________________

How can you begin building that relationship this week? Do you need to show more love? Do you need to tell the person that you love him? Do you need to confess some wrong behavior and ask for his forgiveness? Do you need to forgive him? If you expect God to bless you and your ministry to others, you need to clear up matters at home. How will you begin?

____

____

____

____

____

My Personal Study This Week

- Proverbs 4, 5, and 6. List everything that these Scripture verses teach you about your relationship at home. What instructions should you apply to your life? What wisdom can you glean from this scripture?

A special thanks to Randy Sykes for his inspiration for this chapter.

4

Socializing in Samaria

When you hear the word evangelism, what are the first thoughts that come to your mind? A person preaching? A large crusade with hundreds, maybe thousands of people attending? Handing out tracts on a street? Sharing Christ with a friend?

Evangelism means *communicating the news of Jesus Christ—proclaiming the gospel.* Evangelism isn't just the task of the mass evangelist (one who preaches to large groups). Evangelism, according to the Word, is really the task of every Christian. If we were to take a survey of all the Christians in our world today we would discover that the great majority did not receive Christ through attending a meeting but rather through someone personally leading them to Jesus Christ.

In the next several studies we are going to discover how you can share your faith the way Christ would want you to share it, and in a way that would be tactful and sensitive to people.

A Job for Everyone

For Paul, introducing men and women to Christ was the bottom line of his ministry. In Colossians 1:28 he says, "*So every where we go we talk about Christ to all who will listen.*"

FOUR

HMMMM.

In 2 Timothy 4:1-5, Paul gives his young disciple Timothy some instructions. Specifically, what does Paul tell Timothy, especially in verses 2 and 5? ______________________

____

____

____

It is interesting that evangelism was not considered to be Timothy's spiritual gift (a special ability or strength given by the Holy Spirit), but Paul instructed Timothy to be involved in evangelism anyway. Why? Because God's number-one desire is that people come to know him, and he gives all of us the privilege to be involved.

When we look into God's Word we find that the clearest model of evangelism is Christ himself. John chapter 4 gives us a picture of how Christ himself witnessed, and how he would want you and me to witness also.

Socializing in Samaria

HARUMPH!!!
A SAMARITAN!

WHAT'D
I DO?

Let's begin our study in John 4:3-9, where Jesus and his disciples are traveling from Judea back to Galilee. John tells us that during the course of their journey they passed through a territory called Samaria. The location has great significance for our story.

What do you know about Samaria and the Samaritan people? Verse 9 will help you. ______________________

____

____

Most Jewish people in that day had a serious problem of prejudice when it came to the Samaritan people. In fact, the word Samaritan was a word of contempt with the Jews (John 8:48). Most Jews never even entered Samaria. On their travels they would take the long way and pass around the entire region.

Jesus, of course, was reared as a Jew. He understood why the Jewish people had this particular bias. He understood the implications of traveling through Samaria.

Now besides being a Samaritan, this woman had a specific moral problem. According to verses 16-18, what was this problem? ______________________

____

SOCIALIZING IN SAMARIA

So let's size up the situation. Not only was Jesus talking with a Samaritan, but also with a woman who had serious moral problems. The assumption is that she was a prostitute. Jesus, on the other hand, was perfect. He was holy and righteous, the exact opposite.

If you were to draw a principle from Christ's example thus far, that you could use in your ministry, what would it be?

____

____

____

Wrong Attitudes

Jesus could have handled this situation much differently than he did. He could have avoided the woman. *What would his disciples think* if they came back and found him talking with a Samaritan woman, a woman who was a prostitute? Jesus was also taking a *personal risk* of being rejected. After all, she was a woman of the world. She knew her way around and she was a little cynical.

But Jesus wasn't threatened because someone might not agree with his message. Jesus saw this woman the way he wants you and me to see people, as *someone very special, someone with great spiritual needs.*

As you have been reading, have you recognized some of the wrong attitudes that often creep up in our lives toward those who don't know Christ? List some wrong attitudes toward non-Christians that you have observed among Christians.

____

____

____

____

Why do Christians sometimes have these attitudes?

____

____

____

What are some risks we take when we reach out to someone who does not know Christ? In other words, what might it cost us?

____

____

Have you taken the risk to reach out to somone who didn't know Christ and found it to be well worth it? Tell us about it.

It's Us and Them

I see an attitude among Christians today that kind of bothers me. It's what we could call the "*us and them*" *mentality.*[1] It's a type of ingrown problem that Christians have. It all starts when we see our local gathering of Christians or our church not as a place where we get encouragement and sharpening for sharing our Christian lives in the world but rather as a place where we can find security—kind of like Linus and his blanket. We develop *holy huddles*—*God squads.*

What is most tragic about this problem is that we become less and less sensitive to the needs of non-Christians around us. Consequently, evangelism, if we share at all, is a very *impersonal task.* It is something we will do as a Christian but we will give a big sigh of relief when we are finished. *We witness and run.* Is it any wonder that unbelievers are sometimes uptight when we share?

Getting God's Perspective

For most of us the solution to the *us and them mentality* is saturating our minds with God's perspective. According to these Scripture verses, what is the Lord's attitude toward those who have not yet trusted him with their lives?

2 Peter 3:9

Matthew 9:9-13

Matthew 9:36-38

Luke 19:1-10

SOCIALIZING IN SAMARIA

Jesus never saw people as inconveniences or threats. As far as he was concerned every person that came into his life with a need was a *divine appointment*, set up by his heavenly Father. Have you sensed that God has recently set up a divine appointment for you to share Christ? ____________________

If so, how did you respond? Describe your attitude?

____

____

____

If you were to have this opportunity again, what would you do?

____

____

Becoming All Things

Paul was a great model of one who overcame the *us and them mentality*. In 1 Corinthians 9:19-23, he expresses his attitudes and commitment to those who don't know Christ. What is the main message of this passage?

____

____

____

Paul said he was free from all men, and yet he made himself a *slave* or a *servant* to men. Why did he do this? ____________

____

____

How did he do this? ____________________

____

____

____

Give an example of how you might become a servant to someone in order to win them to Christ. ______________________________

____

____

____

Do you have someone in mind? Who? ______________________

When it comes to Paul's challenge of becoming all things to all men we tend to do one of two things. Either we ignore the challenge and separate ourselves from non-Christians or we overcompensate and try to be so much like them that no one can tell that we are a Christian. (It is amazing how much carnal Christianity is lived out in the name of 1 Corinthians 9:22.)

Paul obviously did not have either of these ideas in mind. *He was talking about freedom to use different methods in relating to people.* Some people he shared with were very religious but did not know how to receive Christ. Others were very secular and worldly and had little knowledge of God. Paul worked hard to relate and identify with people where they were. Think of some non-Christian friends you have and how you would relate to them differently. How could you identify with them and help them identify with you? (*Identify* means to have the same feelings or needs or to put yourself in the other person's place.)

BECOMING ALL THINGS WORK SHEET

My non-Christian friend	*How can I reach out and relate to him/her this week?*

The Conclusion

The first principle we can draw from John 4 is simply this: *God wants us to be available to all people, those who may be like us and those who may be different.*

We have discovered that:
1. Evangelism is a job for everyone.
2. We need to ask God to open our eyes and help us accept people as they are.
3. We need to be a servant to those who have not received Christ.

Putting It All Together

God has asked us all as Christians to be involved in sharing our faith. Why is it a privilege to be involved in God's evangelism?

How would you describe the *us and them* mentality?

What things would you advise a Christian to do to break out of this mentality? What has to change in his attitudes?

"The most significant thing I have learned in this study is:

."

My Action This Week—Writing My Testimony

When Paul shared his faith in Jesus Christ, he often shared his personal experience, his testimony. As you share you will find that being able to verbalize your experience of knowing Christ will help others more clearly understand the Christian life.

In Acts 26, Paul shared his testimony with King Agrippa. Here is how he did it.

- He described his life before he met Christ (vv. 9-11).
- He explained exactly how he came to know Christ (vv. 13-18).
- He described his life once he had received Christ (vv. 19-23).

This week your assignment will be to write out your personal testimony.

To help you communicate clearly, write a paragraph answering each of these questions.

1. Describe your life before you received Christ—your attitudes, your problems (but don't dig out all the dirty laundry; it isn't necessary), the things you were searching for, etc.

2. Explain how and why you became interested in knowing God personally. Explain clearly how you received Christ. Even sharing the words you used when you prayed to receive Christ will help others understand how they can pray to receive Christ.
3. Describe your life since you have received Christ—your attitudes, your perspective on life and on your problems. In what areas has Christ especially made a difference? What are some areas of spiritual growth? How are you changing?

Some important helps for writing your testimony.

- Your testimony should be only three to five minutes long.
- Center your testimony on Jesus, not on yourself—he is the one who is great.
- Use a theme in your testimony. In other words, relate some of the needs Christ has met in question 3 to the needs you had before you received Christ in question 1.
- If you became a Christian as a very young child and question 1 is not really relevant, then emphasize your Christian growth.
- Be creative. Help illustrate your experience by using a story, the words of a song, or perhaps a theme from a movie.
- Avoid words and phrases that are unclear to non-Christians such as "praise the Lord," "born again," "saved," etc. Think of fresh creative ways you can explain these and other truths.
- Share your testimony with another Christian friend, or your group leader. Ask others to help you clarify your communication.

When you have thought through your testimony, you will be prepared and ready to share with anyone at any time. You can also share your testimony at meetings and in your church. Be prepared to share your testimony at your next group meeting.

My Personal Study This Week

- Luke 10:25-37. What was the occupation of the people who were not concerned for the injured man? Describe the attitudes of the Samaritan. What sacrifices did he make for the injured man? What does this Scripture verse teach you about your ministry to others?
- Matthew 9:38; Job 42:10; 1 Samuel 12:23, 24. What do each of these verses teach you about demonstrating a concern for others? What specific things should you be praying for? For whom have you been praying? Do you want to add anyone to your prayer list?

[1]The term *us and them* is used by Rebecca Manley Pippert, the author of the excellent book *Out of the Salt Shaker* (Downers Grove, IL: Inter-Varsity Press, 1979).

5

Uncovering Spiritual Interest

Getting the Right Start

Getting started. Overcoming basic inertia. That is always the biggest problem, isn't it? But once the ball gets rolling our ministry of evangelism can be a genuine adventure. The question is, how do we get started?

Evangelism is not an impersonal technique. It is a very *personal communication* between two people. It is like one beggar who has found food telling another beggar where he can find food also. Evangelism is sharing the most meaningful discovery of one's life. Let's go back to John 4 and the story of Jesus and his visit with the Samaritan woman. Let's see how Jesus pursues his conversation with this woman and how he opens up an opportunity to witness.

In verse 7, what question does Jesus ask? ______________________

____

What other reason, besides being thirsty, could Jesus have had for asking this question? ______________________

____

____

FIVE

I want you to think about something for a moment. Since you have been a Christian, how many times has someone approached you and asked you to help him become a Christian? It has happened to me only once and that was after I had spoken to a group of students on campus. People just do not normally approach us with their spiritual questions and concerns.

Does this mean that they don't have a desire to know God? Not necessarily so. In fact, it's probably just the opposite. I believe every person alive has an inner desire to know the One who created him, and the Holy Spirit uses that desire to create spiritual interest. *You, however, are the one God is going to use to uncover that interest.*

Jesus knew this woman had spiritual needs. He took the initiative to uncover those needs. But he didn't begin by talking about spiritual things. First he was a friend.

The Friendship Factor

In John 4, what did Jesus do that demonstrated his desire to be a friend? ________________________________

____

____

Jesus not only initiated a conversation, he also helped this woman feel important. How did he do this? ________________

____

Jesus had a need—he was thirsty—*so he asked for a favor*. He not only brought up a subject that interested her (water is the whole reason she came to the well), he also made her feel important. *He used his own need to open up an opportunity to meet her need.*

In evangelism we need to learn to talk and care about subjects in which other people are interested. We need to learn how to make people feel important. What are some creative and practical ideas you have that would help you show interest in someone and make him feel important?

____

____

____

____

____

____

Many times we can share Christ with an individual shortly after we meet him, as Jesus did here in John 4. At other times we will have to build a deeper friendship before the person is willing to open to us his spiritual life. *In evangelism it is not either/or—God uses both ways.* As you walk by the Spirit and gain experience you will learn when you need to wait for a person who needs more time to open up.

Arousing Spiritual Curiosity

In his conversation with the Samaritan woman, Jesus had an opportunity to turn his conversation to spiritual issues. How did this opportunity arise? See verse 9. ________________

____

The fact that Jesus initiated a conversation with this woman, and the fact that he was willing to express his need and be friendly really *aroused her curiosity*. She wasn't used to people being this friendly, expecially Jews.

Now when God gives us the opportunity to talk about spiritual truth we need to take action. How does Jesus take action in verse 10?

____

____

____

Jesus did not feel it was necessary to directly address her question (v. 9). (We will talk about answering questions in the next chapter.) Instead he kindled her interest in spiritual issues. *"I have something that you would really be interested in, and, believe it or not, it comes from God."* Jesus knew this woman was spiritually hungry, so he appealed to her need. *He aroused her curiosity.*

Let's think about something. Who are some people you talked with this last week? Do they have spiritual interest? You can be sure they do.

What are some ideas you have that would help uncover spiritual interest in someone? What questions could you ask? What statements could you make? ______________________________

____

____

____

____

____

What are some materials you could give to someone that would arouse spiritual curiosity? ______________________________

____

____

List some events to which you could invite a non-Christian friend that would help uncover spiritual interest and hunger. Think through the different events in your church and the Christian activities in your community and on your campus.

____

____

____

____

The Art of Asking Questions

Questions were the ultimate method that Jesus used to help people think and to arouse their spiritual interest. Questions focus the attention on the person you want to share with, and they help *him* express *his* thoughts and feelings.

The key to asking questions is listening. If you are a good listener you can pick up at the point of the person's need, and turn the conversation to Jesus Christ. *If you will listen, the person will be ready to listen to you.*

There are a lot of different questions we can use to help people open up. Questions can focus on such things as a discussion in one of your classes, what your friend believes and why (and don't be critical of their answers), a personal problem someone may have, or a problem on campus, a current event, or someone's philosophy of life.

What are some questions you could ask that would help you discern a person's thinking and needs, and give you an opportunity to share? ______________________

____

____

____

____

____

Putting It All Together

We have learned from John 4 that we need to take the initiative to:

1. Show interest in people and build friendships.
2. Arouse spiritual curiosity and uncover spiritual interest.

Why is it important that we demonstrate friendship to those who need Christ? ______________________

____

____

____

____

Jesus was always concerned about people's needs. This is what opened up his opportunities to witness. Using the following work sheets, think through your concern for others.

FRIENDSHIP WORK SHEET 1

Non-Christians I have seen in the last several days	*What needs does he or she have?*

FRIENDSHIP WORK SHEET 2

My non-Christian friend or acquaintance	*What materials could I give him/her that would arouse spiritual interest? What activity could I invite him/her to?*

How would you recognize someone who is spiritually hungry and open? ______________________________

____

____

____

Do you know of someone like this right now? __________

Who? ______________________________

My Action This Week—Taking the Initiative

Here are two assignments for you to complete this week.

1. Here is something that will help you realize that you really can take the initiative and relate to people. Each day this week, strike up a conversation with a person who is a stranger or someone you don't know well. Your only objective will be to get to know something about that person. Be ready to share your experiences at your next group meeting, sharing some of the things about the people you meet—what they do, their interests, etc.
2. Decide on two people (from your worksheet) with whom you want to take the initiative this week. How will you show interest in them? What will you do to create spiritual interest—invite them to a meeting or give them some contemporary material to read?

Sources for contemporary material for evangelism: *Campus Crusade for Christ*, High School and College Ministries (Arrowhead Springs, San Bernardino, CA 92414.); *Young Life* (720 West Monument Street, Colorado Springs, CO 80901; *Youth For Christ* (P.O. Box 419, Wheaton, IL 60187); *Issues and Answers Newspaper* (Student Action for Christ, P.O. Box 608, Herrin, IL 62948); *Student Impact* (P.O. Box 26486, San Diego, CA 92126).

My Personal Study This Week

- Matthew 14:13-23. What was Jesus' attitude toward people, even when he was tired and needed rest? How did God the Father bless his attitude? What truth from this passage will I apply to my life?
- Matthew 9:35-38. Describe Jesus' attitudes toward others in this passage. For what should I be concerned? For what should I pray?
- Acts 4:1-22. What does this passage teach me about sharing my faith? Why can I be confident when I share? How should I respond to someone who might oppose me? What role does the Holy Spirit play in my life as I share?

6

Making the Message Clear

One of the remarks I hear from people with whom I share Christ is: "I never understood Christianity like this before. Now it's clear!"

They are talking about the misconceptions that once clouded their minds. Most people see Christianity as a religion of dos and don'ts, most of which they perceive as impossible to follow. They do not see Christianity as a relationship with Christ. *Our job is to make the truth of Christianity clear.*

In this study we are going to discover the logical progression that Jesus used in communicating spiritual truth.

Principle #1: The Positive Approach

As we look at the way Jesus communicated the gospel we will see that he followed a progression of *four* specific principles. The first principle or point he wanted to make with the woman at the well is found in John 4:10, 13 and 14. What do you see as significant about the *way* Jesus opened their conversation on spiritual truth?

____

____

Jesus knew that this woman had serious moral, sexual problems. He could have come down on her really hard. But instead *he chose to be positive.* How? By offering her something that, deep down, she really wanted—satisfaction, a solution to her restless life.

The message of evangelism is a positive message, and so we need to be positive. Yes, we need to make the issue of sin and separation from God very clear, but the way that we turn the conversation to spiritual truth is by *being positive.*

Discuss some positive statements you could use to introduce spiritual truth. ____________________

____

____

____

____

What are some negative statements we should avoid?

____

____

____

____

MAKING THE MESSAGE CLEAR

Here are some Scripture passages that will help you be positive in your message. John 3:16; 10:10; Romans 5:1, 8; 1 John 4:9, 10. What others would you add?

Principle #2: Defining the Problem

In verses 16-18 Jesus turns the conversation again. What do you think Jesus is communicating to the woman?

____

____

In evangelism, why is it essential that we discuss sin?

____

____

____

People are not always going to feel comfortable when we talk about sin and morals. But unless the problem of sin is understood there cannot be any real understanding of why Christ died on the cross. Nor is there an understanding of repentance—a willingness by anyone to turn from a self-centered life-style and let God change him or her.

Let's think about this. How would you define sin to someone with whom you were sharing Christ?

____

____

____

____

When explaining sin, how would you explain Romans 3:23 and 6:23? ______________________________

____

____

Romans 5:12? ______________________________

____

This definition of sin may be helpful to you:
Man was created to find fellowship and meaning in a relationship with God. But because of his independent self-will he chose to go his own way and find meaning apart from God. Consequently his relationship with God was broken. This self-will is characterized by attitudes of both rebellion and indifference toward God, and is an evidence of what the Bible calls sin.[1]

What do you especially like about this definition? ____________

You will want to memorize the basic points of this definition so that you are prepared as you communicate Christ to others.

Principle #3: God's Solution

In verse 20 the Samaritan woman asks Jesus a question concerning ultimate religious truth and where and how God can be found. (At the end of this chapter there is a section on how to answer questions as we share our faith.) Christ lets the woman herself come to a conclusion. What does she say in verse 25?

____

Although I am sure her knowledge was very limited on religious matters, she knew that this one called the Christ was the ultimate truth. She had no idea she was talking to him but she was hungry to know him. So Jesus pointed her directly to himself (v. 26). *He was the issue.*

Why, in your opinion, is it *absolutely essential* that we make Christ the center of our discussion in our evangelism?

____

____

____

MAKING THE MESSAGE CLEAR

In evangelism it can be easy to get off the track and talk about issues that really don't lead people to Christ. We can talk about philosophies, theology, politics, ourselves, our church denomination, none of which get to the issue of receiving Christ.

Paul was very mindful of this as he shared his faith. In your own words, explain what he tells us.

2 Corinthians 4:5.

1 Corinthians 2:1-5.

According to verse 5, why did these people make solid decisions for Christ?

In your ministry, how could you make sure that people do not get a wrong concept of what it means to be a Christian?

Making the Solution Clear

... ALL THAT IS INTERESTING. BUT THE BASIC ISSUE IS THE PERSON OF JESUS AND THE SIGNIFICANCE OF HIS DEATH AND RESURRECTION.

Christ's *death on the cross*, his *resurrection*, and the fact that he is *the only way to God* are the *essentials* of our message. We put our faith in Christ on the basis of these truths.

When talking about Christ, what do these Scripture verses help you communicate?

1 Timothy 2:5, 6 and John 14:6?

Romans 5:8?

1 Corinthians 15:3-8?

YOU MEAN IT ALL BOILS DOWN TO WHETHER OR NOT I AM WILLING TO BELIEVE THAT JESUS IS WHO HE SAYS HE IS? THAT DECISION HAS A LOT OF IMPLICATIONS...
LIKE FREEDOM.

Let's move in our study of Jesus' style of evangelism.

Principle #4: Asking for a Response

In John 4:26, Jesus is really posing a question to this woman. What do you think he is saying?

I find that as I share my faith most people expect me to ask them to receive Christ. It would be strange if I didn't.

Don't be surprised if asking people to receive Christ seems a little difficult. Bringing up the subject of sin and asking people to receive Christ are the most difficult areas of evangelism. For one thing, we are sort of confronting people, and none of us like to do that. Second, Satan, the enemy, is furious when we ask people to receive Christ, and he is going to *try* to make it difficult for us.

Jesus, in verse 26, is in essence asking this woman to accept him as the Christ, the one she talked of in verse 25. "*I am the one you are looking for,*" says Jesus. "*Are you willing to accept that? Are you willing to receive me as your Messiah?*" And she did.

In asking someone to receive Christ, what do these verses help you communicate?

Matthew 4:17? ______

John 1:12? ______

John 3:1-8? ______________________________

Ephesians 2:8, 9? ______________________________

Here are the key truths to remember when explaining how to receive Christ.

- To receive Christ we must *admit our need of him and his forgiveness.* We do this through prayer—talking with God.
- We must be willing to turn from our old life-style and let God change us—*repentance.* (This is why Jesus asked the Samaritan woman to go and get her husband.) *We must surrender our will to Christ.*
- We receive Christ by *faith.* This means that we trust him to save us and enter our lives by his Spirit. Faith is an act of our will, not just intellectual agreement with the truth.

Letting the Holy Spirit Work

How hard do you think we should push people to make a decision for Christ? ______________________________

In asking for a response, how does Jesus handle the Samaritan woman? Does he push her? ______________________________

According to John 16:7, 8, whose job is it to convince people that they should receive Christ? ______________________________

What, then, is our job? ______________________________

If your friend says *yes,* I want to receive Christ, then explain to him how he can express his desire to God through prayer. Help him by explaining to him what prayer is (talking to God), and suggest what he might say. Then pray with him.

If your friend says, "No, I'm not ready to receive Christ," answer any more questions he may have and continue to be a warm and available friend. Many people receive Christ further down the road as the Holy Spirit makes their need more obvious to them and as we continue to be available.

At the end of this chapter I have included a section called *Using Tools.* You will want to read through this to see what tools will help you as you share Christ.

Putting It All Together

Christ's discussion with the Samaritan woman followed a logical progression of four specific truths.

1. Verse 10—*God's plan for man is fulfillment and meaning.* What specific truth was communicated in each of these verses in John 4?
2. Verses 16-18? ______
3. Verse 25? ______
4. Verse 26? ______

Why is it important to be clear when sharing Christ?

______

How would you define sin? ______

______

Why is it important that we ask people to receive Christ?

______

What would you do if your friend said "Yes, I want to receive Christ"? ______

______

What would you do if he did *not* want to receive Christ?

______

Using Tools

One way you can help make your message clear to others is by using tools—simple materials designed to help you share Christ. You will find that many evangelistic tools are patterned after the way Jesus shared the truth in John 4.
Here are some tools that will help you.

- *So You Want Solutions* (Wheaton, IL: Tyndale House, 1979). This is especially good for those who are interested in Christ, but want to study more about him before they make a decision.
- *The Four Spiritual Laws* (Campus Crusade for Christ, San Bernardino, CA 92414).
- *Steps to Peace with God* (Billy Graham Evangelistic Assoc., Minneapolis, MN).
- There are many other good tools available too numerous to list. Tools and materials are designed to be your servant. They don't control you. You control them. You will find that they make things clear and help you to stay on track.

Answering Questions

As we share our faith we always want to be available to answer questions. *Evangelism is not cramming information down people's throats. It is helping people understand spiritual truth.*

The key to answering questions is knowing when to stop and camp on a question and when to pull stakes and move on toward your objective—communicating Jesus Christ. In our story in John 4 Jesus stopped and answered some questions (vv. 20-24), and others he passed over because he knew that the woman really wasn't that concerned about the answer (v. 9).

If you aren't sure of the sincerity of someone's question you might ask him this question: *"If you knew the answer to that question would it help you make a decision to become a Christian?"* If the answer is *yes*, then answer it as best you can. Be honest if you don't know the answer and tell him you will try to find out.

OH YES, THIS REALLY IS A QUESTION THAT I'VE BEEN THINKING ABOUT.
WELL, I'LL GIVE IT SOME THOUGHT AND TRY TO ANSWER IT FOR YOU...

If his answer is *no*, or if he hedges, assure him that most of his questions will be answered as you continue to explain how to become a Christian. And you will find that nearly all questions do take care of themselves as you help people understand how to receive Christ.

Discuss some questions that people may ask and how you might answer them.

These books will give you help for answering questions.

Answers to Tough Questions by Josh McDowell (available from Here's Life Publishers, Box 1576, San Bernardino, CA 92402).

More Than a Carpenter by Josh McDowell (Wheaton, IL: Tyndale House Publishers, 1977).

Know Why You Believe by Paul E. Little (Wheaton, IL: Victor Books, 1970).

My Action This Week—Sharing My Faith

Your assignment this week will be to trust God for an opportunity to share Christ with one individual. Who have you been getting to know with whom you need to share Christ? Think about this and pray about it. You decide when and how you will share with them.

My Personal Study This Week

- 2 Corinthians 4:1-10. What does this teach me about making the message clear? What does it teach me about personal motives, about enduring hardship, and about eternal values? What do I need to apply to my life from this Scripture passage?
- John 21:1-14. What does this passage teach me about obedience to Jesus, especially in reaching people? Why were the disciples successful at catching fish? Why will I be successful at winning people to Christ?
- Acts 8:25-39. In which verses did Philip demonstrate the qualities of knowledge of God's Word, compassion, obedience to God, humility, enthusiasm, tactfulness, boldness, sensitivity to the Spirit's guidance? What principles in this story will you apply to your witnessing ministry?

[1]Some of the ideas for this definition of sin came from Campus Crusade's *Four Spiritual Laws*.

7

Taking the Initiative

Jesus was never satisfied with just news-weather-sports type relationships. His commitment to people was much deeper. He was always aware of needs—eternal needs, and as God's Spirit works in each of our lives, these are the issues we will become concerned with also. *Are we willing to take the initiative to meet these needs?*

We have discovered how to uncover spiritual interest in our friends, and how to make the gospel message clear when we share. Now let's dig in and talk about some communication skills as well as some attitudes that will help us *take the initiative* to share our faith.

Spiritual Shyness

Have you ever had an experience something like this? While you are talking with a friend, the subject of his personal needs comes up (or something else is said that could lead to an opportunity to share Christ), and you just stand there with your tongue tied in one big knot. You don't know what to say. And isn't this especially true with people you have known for a long time? You can talk about anything except. . . .

Why, in your opinion, is it sometimes difficult to talk with others about spiritual things? ______________________

____

____

____

THERE SEEMS TO BE NO PURPOSE IN LIFE... WHAT DO YOU THINK?
....MMMPHGRPLE...

Sometimes this difficulty is a result of our own embarrassment. Paul says we should not be embarrassed or timid. Why? See Romans 1:16, 17.

____

____

What resource do we have to overcome our embarrassment and fear? See Acts 4:8 and 2 Timothy 1:7, 8.

____

____

Discuss briefly in your group how one can be filled with the Holy Spirit and walk in the Spirit. Record the insights that help you.

____

____

____

Being Casual but Definite

In John 4 we have a vivid picture of how to take the initiative when sharing our faith. Jesus became a friend and he casually but definitely turned the attention of the Samaritan woman to her spiritual needs.

At the same time Jesus was not *heavy and preachy.* We certainly do not need to be preachy with our friends either. We can relax. The Holy Spirit is at work in the lives of our friends and we are only *his mouthpiece–his communicator.* We are *God's messenger boy* and as we witness in the power of the Spirit we can leave the results to God.[1]

Why, in your opinion, would it turn people off if we were to preach intensely at them?

___

___

___

When Jesus shared he was casual but definite. What do you think it means to be *casual but definite?*

___

___

___

According to John 16:8, Mark 13:11, and Acts 1:8, why can we relax in the Holy Spirit when we share our faith? Be specific.

___

___

___

Clear Communication

Not only should we be casual but definite in our witness, we should also be clear in our communication. Do you use *Christian lingo* or *God talk* when you share? I have heard Christians enthusiastically try to explain spiritual truth to non-Christians by using terms and clichés such as, *praise the Lord, saved, born again, God blesses you* and a host of others that the non-Christian did not understand. These terms are meaningful to Christians, but are unclear to unbelievers.

As good communicators we need to be fresh and creative in explaining spiritual truth. We can explain what it means to have a relationship with Christ and power to be a new person. Then we can explain that this is what is meant by being born again. *We need to translate Christian terms.*

Discuss in your group how you could freshly and creatively explain each of these terms to a non-Christian: *Born again, God blesses you, saved, sin, grace, inviting Christ into your life, receive Christ,* the *abundant life, fellowship.* There may be others that you want to add.

Reacting or Responding

OK... HOW DO YOU KNOW THIS IS TRUE?

Relaxing in the Spirit and clearly communicating are important in our witness to others. But what happens if someone does not relax with us, and in fact reacts when we try to share our faith?

Let's return to our story in John 4. In verses 10-14 Jesus turns his conversation with the Samaritan woman from a request for water to an offer for living water—inner satisfaction. He turned the conversation to spiritual issues. At first the woman wanted to challenge Christ's claim to have the answers to life (vv. 11, 12): "How can you know the truth? No one knows for sure." This is not unusual. Some people may respond this way, even after we have established a friendship.

Has anyone ever said this to you? How would you answer in a way that would help someone come to Christ?

____

____

____

What do you think is significant about the way Christ answered the Samaritan woman in verses 13, 14? ________________

____

____

There are three ways we could respond to someone who questions us as the Samaritan woman questioned Jesus.

1. We could back off, retreat, and give up.
2. We could react or argue, trying to impress people with what we know.
3. We can respond positively.

Why do you think it is important not to argue with people when we share Christ? ________________

____

____

Discuss these Scripture verses. What do they tell us about attitudes as we witness? 2 Timothy 2:23-26, Galatians 5:25, 26.

Attitudes we should have	*Attitudes we should avoid*

Many people who are unhappy and dissatisfied with life are a little argumentative, as was this woman. But as we continue in our study we will see *she did not want Jesus to back off and leave her alone.* People who challenge us seldom do. In fact, they are disappointed if we do retreat. "Well, I guess he's not that convinced himself."

Jesus kept his focus on her real need, not her reactions, and it helped him to continue to relate.

An Example of Taking the Initiative

In Acts 17:16-34, Paul gives us a practical demonstration of taking the initiative and effectively relating to the secular non-Christian people of his day. List the principles and insights you see in this passage that will help you as you relate to non-Christians. Was Paul casual but definite (list the verses)? What does he say to respond rather than to react? How does he turn the conversation to Christ? How does he make the message clear? How would you describe his results? Be specific. Give verses along with your principles and findings.

Attitudes for Taking the Initiative

As we wrap up our study I want you to think about your responsibility of taking advantage of opportunities to share Christ. You have to take the step of faith. No one can do that for you.

Here are some suggestions that will help you *take the initiative.*

1. *Pray specifically for opportunities to share Christ.* One of the biggest reasons we don't share our faith is because we are not spiritually or mentally prepared. We are not really thinking about or praying for our friends.
2. *Consider the immense importance of someone knowing Christ.* Don't take other people's salvation lightly. God doesn't. He made the greatest sacrifice of all time—on the cross. Ask God to give you a heart of compassion. Take your mind off all the temporal things of the world and focus your attention on what really matters—eternal values. These Scripture verses will help you: Matthew 9:36-39; Romans 10:13-15; 1 Timothy 2:1-4, 2 Corinthians 4:16—5:10.
3. *Don't be afraid of failure.* It has been said, "He who never fails never does anything." I think that speaks for itself.

TAKING THE INITIATIVE

4. *Look for opportunities.* If you have asked God for an opportunity to share then expect it. Your friend may ask a question, express a personal need, or give an opinion, hoping you will respond. Be on the alert. When your opportunity comes be *casual but definite.* In other words, relax. God is in control. But take the initiative. Step into your opportunity.
5. *Create opportunities.* When people were not coming to Jesus he went to them. *This is the most important and exciting part of your ministry.* I like to create opportunities by setting up a special time for a Coke or inviting a person to a meeting or Bible study where Christ will be discussed. Have your friend over for dinner.

   When creating opportunities always be very honest as to why you would like to get together. Explain that you have discovered something that has really helped the spiritual dimension of your life and say that you think it would interest them also. What are some creative things you could do to create an opportunity to share Christ? ____________

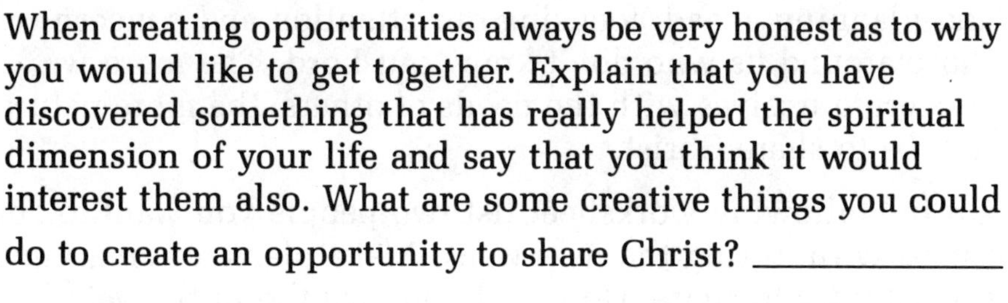

6. *Teamwork.* Perhaps you could *pair up* with a Christian friend and *pray together* for those with whom you want to share (Matthew 18:19). You could also create opportunities together—team evangelism (Luke 10:1).

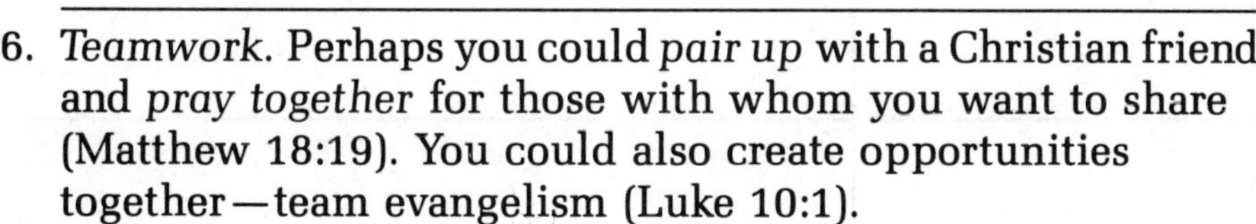

Putting It All Together

We have discovered that as we share our faith we need to:
- Take the initiative.
- Be casual but definite.
- Relax in the Spirit.
- Be clear when we use biblical and Christian terms.
- Do not argue with those with whom we share.

Share with your group your experience of sharing your faith this last week.

In our last three studies we have taken a good look at Jesus' witness in John 4. What has been the most significant truth you have learned from these studies?

What is the most significant principle for sharing that you discovered in Paul's witness in Act's 17:16-34? How can you apply this principle to your sharing opportunities this week?

____

____

____

____

My Action This Week

LORD, GIVE ME THE OPPORTUNITY TO TALK WITH JILL TODAY!

Sharing our faith is something that God wants as a regular part of our lives. Successful sharing is really a way of life.

But for sharing to become a way of life we need to be thinking and planning ahead, focusing our attention and concern on those around us who don't know our Lord. The more we concern ourselves with the needs of others, the more natural it will be to share Christ.

On the following worksheet list two people you want to share Christ with during the next week. Make plans for creating an opportunity to share. How will you take the initiative?

My non-Christian friend	*How can I create an opportunity to share Christ? When will I do this?*

My Personal Study This Week

- Luke 5:17-26. What did these men do to demonstrate their determination to get their friend to Jesus? Why did Jesus heal their friend? What does this passage teach you about taking the initiative?
- 2 Timothy 3:14—4:8. What are Paul's challenges to Timothy? In what ways does Paul challenge Timothy to take the initiative? How can you apply this to your life?

[1]The term "Share Christ in the power of the Holy Spirit and leave the results to God" is used by Campus Crusade for Christ in their evangelism training (Arrowhead Springs, San Bernardino, CA 92414).

8

Serving Young Christians

In a way, being a spiritual reproducer is like being married and deciding whether or not to have children. Without children life may be a little more simple, and for sure there are less demands. Having children is definitely more work, but the dividends are nothing short of great!

Having spiritual children (introducing people to Christ) is really the same. It is going to cost you something to be a spiritual reproducer. You must learn to *serve*, be a *friend*, and *train*, but the dividends are rich. There are few things in life more gratifying than watching a young Christian grow.

In this study we are going to discuss how you can follow up on new Christians.

The young Christians we follow up on and disciple are *God's workmanship, his building under construction,* just as you and I are under construction (Ephesians 2:10, Philippians 1:6). We are just God's fellow workers. Our only responsibility is to *trust Christ* and be where God wants us to be—*serving people.*

EIGHT

Being a Servant

A servant, as defined in the dictionary, is a person who is in the *service of another,* someone who *renders assistance and help,* one who is *of use to another.* Young Christians need a servant.

Let's stop for a moment and consider just where a new Christian is coming from. What do you think are the most critical needs in a new Christian's life? ______________________________

____

____

____

A young believer has some transitions to go through. He has left the kingdom of this world with all its twisted values and has stepped into God's kingdom. He has become a new creation (2 Corinthians 5:17), with a new life-style to which he must adjust, a life-style of faith in Christ rather than in himself. He definitely needs a servant, someone who will *guide* him along the way.

Two Ways to Lead

As Jesus trained his disciples he taught them that there were two ways to lead others. In Mark 10:42-45 Jesus describes these two types of leadership. What are they?

Which style of leadership were his disciples to use?

Why do you think this style of leadership is so much more effective than the other, especially when leading young Christians?

Is it more demanding to be a leader who serves rather than a leader who uses his authority? Why? What might it cost you to be a servant-leader?

List several specific ways you could be a servant to a young Christian.

The measure of your spiritual leadership is not determined by the number you rule over but by the number you serve.

DOWN!
DOWN & LISTEN!
...MIKE, I'D LIKE TO HELP YOU OUT IN YOUR RELATIONSHIP WITH CHRIST. WE CAN LEARN TOGETHER.
UNDER CONSTRUCTION

Attitudes of a Servant

In 1 Peter 5:2-5, Peter talks of the attitudes we must have if we are going to shepherd (serve and lead) other Christians. These instructions were given to the elders of the church and they are the attitudes we must have also as we begin to minister to young Christians.

In this Scripture passage there are at least four attitudes that we need to cultivate as we serve other Christians. Can you find them? List your findings. ______

______

______

______

______

What are some of the wrong attitudes mentioned here that we are to avoid? ______

______

______

Why would these attitudes hurt our ministry to young Christians?

______

______

Verse 3 says that we are to prove to be an *example.* What are some things you should demonstrate as an example to young Christians? ______

______

______

______

______

Building Friendships

Servanthood is greatly enhanced by *friendship.* Young Christians need a close friend who will encourage them, be listeners, and include them in the body of Christ.

Paul talks about the close friendships he had with young Christians in Thessalonica. What does Paul tell us in 1 Thessalonians 2:5-8?

What two very important things did Paul share with these people?

What do you think it means to share our lives? Give some examples.

Why would a strong friendship help you to be effective as you teach and train a young Christian?

Let's Start Building

As you follow up new Christians, what are some specific ways that you could build relationships? You might ask yourself, "If I had just received Christ, how would I want someone to build a relationship with me?"

Here are some ideas for building relationships that have worked well for others. Compare them to your ideas.

- *Be available.* Learn to be a listener. It communicates an attitude of acceptance.

HEY! WOULDN'T YOU LIKE TO JOIN US? . . . C'MON!!!

- *Learn to be an encourager.* Learn to think the best of others.
- *Show special kindnesses. Learn to be a giver,* of your time and your possessions.
- *Find out what their interests are* and do the things they want to do. Put them before yourself.
- *Go places together.* If you are planning any kind of activity—shopping, recreation, doing some work for someone—give your new Christian friend a call and ask him to go along.
- *Phone them.* Let them know you are thinking about them.
- *Exercise and work out together.*
- *Study together*—schoolwork and Bible study.
- *Eat together.* Go out for meals or a pizza. Eating is a great time to have fellowship, a great time to talk.
- *Invite them over for dinner.* Let them get to know your family.
- *Attend Christian activities together.* Select meetings that will be helpful for their growth. Involve them in your church.
- *Write them,* especially when you are out of town on a trip. Let them know how you are doing and that you are thinking of them.

- *Share personally what God is teaching you.* Don't be afraid to share some of your own needs.

If someone loves you he will also love your message. Friendship opens the door for teaching and training others.
Friendship–follow-up will never work without it.

Putting It All Together

We have discovered that the spiritual growth of a young Christian is the work of the Holy Spirit. What are your responsibilities in a young Christian's life?

Why is it critical to be a servant and friend to a new Christian?

In your opinion, how could your friendship with new Christians be instrumental in helping others come to know Christ? (Compare your answer to John 13:34, 35.)

"The most significant thing I have learned in this study is:

."

My Action This Week—Being a Servant

This week your assignment will be to begin building a relationship with a young Christian. *Remember that beginning a ministry of follow-up does not mean that we stop sharing with unbelievers.* Continue to share Christ with others and recruit other Christian friends to help with the follow-up.

Who are one or more young Christians you need to build a relationship with this week? (It is best for guys to work with guys and girls with girls.)

In what specific ways will you begin building a friendship with this individual or individuals? ______________________

____

____

____

____

When and how will you get in touch with your young Christian friend? ______________________

____

What will you say to him? How will you explain your purpose for getting together? ______________________

____

____

____

____

This week concentrate mainly on friendship. You will also want to review with him the Scriptures on assurance of salvation. Romans 10:13; 1 John 5:12, 13; John 1:12; 5:24; Colossians 1:13, 14. In our next study we will discuss what to teach a young Christian.

Be ready to share your experiences at your next meeting.

My Personal Study This Week

- Acts 20:28-38. Describe Paul's attitudes toward these Christians. What does this passage teach you about caring for Christians? What are the results of caring for Christians?
- Matthew 13:3-9, 18-23. What happened to the seed planted in each of the soils? The four soils represent the responses to God's Word—the seed. What are these responses and how could you share them with a new Christian to motivate him to spiritual growth?
- 1 Thessalonians 5:12-19. What attitudes should you have toward those over you and those to whom you minister?

I'M YOUR
SERVANT...FRIEND...& TEACHER.

9

Building Young Christians

Not only does a young Christian need a friend and a servant, he also needs a teacher, someone who will instruct him and build him up in the basics of the Christian life. You can teach others what you have learned, *and you can also learn together.*

Growing Christians

In the first chapter of Colossians, Paul expressed his desire to help young Christians grow. Paul took new believers very seriously. He knew that young Christians were greatly affected by those who loved them or refused to love them, those who would get involved with them or refused to get involved.

In Colossians 1:28, Paul shares the three objectives he had in his ministry to young Christians. Can you pick out these three aims or objectives?

____

____

____

Of these three, which was the ultimate aim?

____

What do you think it means to present someone *complete* or *perfect* in Christ? ______________________________

____

____

THE
GOAL

How did Paul accomplish this task? What does this teach you? (See v. 29.) ______

______

______

______

What Do You Mean, "Complete"?

When Paul uses the word *perfect or complete* in Colossians 1:28, he is talking about *maturity*—in this case spiritual maturity as opposed to immaturity. The significance of Paul's usage of these words is that he had a *goal* in mind, something he was aiming for. He knew that Christians could grow and mature, so he wasn't satisfied with just a hit and miss ministry. He wanted something very specific to result from his time invested with these young Christians.

In the same way we need a goal in our ministry, something we are trusting God to do in the lives of those we are leading.

In Ephesians 4:11-16, Paul talked about some of the qualities he knew would become visible in the life of a growing Christian. The development of these qualities were some of the goals he trusted God for as he worked with young Christians. List as many of these qualities of growth as you can find.

____

____

____

____

____

____

Relational Thinking vs. Terminal Thinking

Setting your goals and then organizing your ministry to reach those goals, as Paul did, is what we call *relational thinking*. It means that we relate what we do to how it will help us reach our objective. *You always know why you are doing what you are doing.*

Terminal thinking, on the other hand, is going about your activities without any real plan in mind. You do things, *but you don't know why you do them,* or how they relate to helping you reach your goals. They are terminal activities—an end in themselves.

Terminal thinking is like taking a number of boards, nailing them together, and hoping that if you nail long enough, and put in enough effort, your work will result in some type of building. You don't have a plan but you are keeping busy. How would you like to have a terminal thinker build your house?

A relational thinker, on the other hand, will go to the blueprint, take a look at a picture of the finished product, and then follow the plans that will help him put together the finished product—your new house.

If we are going to help build up young believers we need to be *relational thinkers*. We need to go about our God-given task *with an objective in mind,* and *a plan* to reach that objective. Once we know what God wants to accomplish in someone's life, our job is to be a co-worker with God, helping develop those things.

Learning to Be Relational

Let's take some time to think about your ministry. How can you be a relational thinker? From here on out you are going to have to do a good deal of thinking, so get ready to dig in.

Let's say you have been working with a young Christian for a number of months building a friendship with him and teaching him the basics of the Christian life. List four or five *qualities* or *characteristics* in his life that would indicate that he is a growing Christian.

Now let's think about this. *What would you teach him* that would help him grow spiritually in these areas? Include any Scripture verse you might think of.

Just teaching truth is not going to be enough to help this young Christian grow. *What activities* would you want him to be involved in that would help him grow and develop in the areas you previously listed? Include more than just activities to attend. Include things you want him to *do*. Be sure you know why this activity helps him. Lots of times we do activities just for activities' sake.

WE'LL BE CLEANING UP MRS. SMITH'S YARD TODAY.... THIS IS PART OF BEING INVOLVED IN "MINISTRY".

So far your young Christian friend has been exposed to teaching and activities, but he also needs to see the Christian life in action. Paul said, "Follow my example, just as I follow Christ's" (1 Corinthians 11:1). In what areas should you be an *example*?

If it has been difficult for you to answer these questions, don't be discouraged. As you gain experience in working with young Christians, you will become more effective as a relational thinker. The important thing is to begin to understand what you want to trust God to accomplish in your ministry and what he wants *you* to do.

Understanding Needs

Everything that a young believer needs to learn from the Scriptures is not to be taught to him all at once. It would blow his mind. So we need to start at the beginning and build.

Here are perhaps the *most important truths* that a young believer needs to learn.

1. He needs the *assurance* that if he has received Christ, that Christ is in his life, and that he will not leave him (Hebrews 13:5-8).
2. He needs to understand that he is now a *new creation* in Jesus Christ. He now has a *new identity* and he is going to find meaning in life as he trusts and obeys Christ (2 Corinthians 5:17).
3. He needs a growing *knowledge of Jesus Christ.* As he learns more about the uniqueness of Jesus, he will develop a stronger faith (John 20:31; Romans 10:17).
4. He needs to understand the *forgiveness* he has in Jesus Christ, and how to confess his sins as a Christian (Romans 5:6-9; 1 John 1:9).
5. He needs to understand and experience the *power* he now has to live a new life because of *Christ's resurrection* (1 Corinthians 15:14-19; Galatians 2:20).
6. He needs to understand the *ministry of the Holy Spirit* in his life (John 14:25, 26; Ephesians 5:18).
7. He needs to learn how to *pray* and how to *study his Bible.* (2 Timothy 3:16, 17; Philippians 4:6, 7).
8. He needs to become part of a *local body of believers* (Hebrews 10:25).
9. He needs to learn how to *share his faith* with those who have not received Christ (Romans 10:13-15).

A Teacher and His Tools

You are probably asking yourself, "How can I possibly know enough to teach all of these things?"

To help you to be both effective and organized as you teach, it would be profitable to use a study manual entitled *So You Want Solutions.* This tool is designed to help a young Christian in his spiritual growth. Each week you can discuss a new chapter and that way be assured that your disciple is being taught the truths from God's Word that you want him to learn.

So You Want Solutions and the leader's guide, *So You Want to Lead Students,* are both available at your Christian bookstore, or you can order them from Tyndale House Publishers, Box 80, Wheaton, IL 60187.

Let's Get Started

So now it's time to get started. If you have someone you have led to Christ, or if it is your responsibility to help a young believer in his spiritual growth, follow these guidelines.

1. When someone has become a Christian, *get together with him as soon as possible,* preferably within twenty-four to forty-eight hours. Don't allow new Christians to go uncared for.
2. When setting up your follow-up appointments, *you suggest a place and time*, and let him or her respond. Adjust to his or her schedule if necessary.
3. When you get together, *personalize your time.* Ask questions that focus the attention on him or her, not on you.
   - Discover his or her interests.
   - What motivated him or her to receive Christ?
   - If he or she has been a Christian for a while, ask the person to share some of the things that have happened in his or her life since receiving Christ.
   - Would he or she like to grow as a Christian?
   - You should be willing to meet with this person on a regular basis to help him or her as a Christian. You are growing also and you could grow together. Would he or she like to meet with you?

I'D LIKE TO HELP YOU.
WE CAN STUDY AND
LEARN TOGETHER...
WHAT DO YOU THINK?

4. *Review the assurance* the person has of knowing Christ (Romans 10:13; 1 John 5:12, 13; John 1:12; 5:24; Hebrews 13:5-8).
5. Show him the *material* you are going to study and give him a copy. Explain that you would like to meet with him or her as long as he or she would like, but at least long enough to complete the first five chapters of *So You Want Solutions*. When you have completed the first five chapters you can challenge him or her to a new commitment to meet six more times and complete the book.
6. Get together for your study time *at least once a week*. If something happens and you can't get together at the scheduled time, reschedule your appointment within forty-eight hours. Don't leave a young Christian unattended.

7. Of course, follow-up is not just studying. Talk about something you can do that week—recreation, church, etc.
8. When you meet for your study time:
   - Have a sharing time—everyone should share.
   - Bible study time—discuss your lesson together.
   - Question time—try to answer any questions that may come up.
   - Pray together—conversationally. Be simple.

The size of your growth group or follow-up group can be anywhere from one to ten or even more. However, the best groups usually do not exceed four or five members. The smaller the group the easier it is for you to be a personal friend to each new Christian. Just working with one or two new believers would be a good way to start.

An Environment for Growth

As we have discovered before, the power to accomplish the ministry that God has given us comes from his Spirit. Our responsibility is to be hard, smart workers, and God's Spirit will use us in the lives of people (Psalm 127:1; 1 Corinthians 3:5-9).

So what happens if someone does not grow as fast as we had anticipated? Should we prod him along? Should we really let him have it? God's Spirit works *differently* in each one of our lives. One person may grow faster than another. *We cannot control that growth.* You will want to continually encourage your young Christian friends to apply what they are learning; but beyond that, the person's growth is between God and himself. *Your prayer* will have infinitely more power in his life than anything else you do.

Putting It All Together

Describe how you were followed up after you became a Christian, or if you were not followed up personally, describe what helped you most in your initial growth? ____________

____

____

____

____

____

What is terminal thinking? Give your own original example.

What is relational thinking, and why would it help you to be effective as you minister to others?

What should you do to help a young Christian who:

- Has some bad habits from his old life?

- Is not responding to your desire to get together for follow-up?

- Has no other Christian friends?

As you begin a ministry of follow-up you will probably encounter one or more of the *following problems* creeping up in your attitudes. For each problem think through some solutions as to how you could deal with that problem. Find Scripture verses that apply to solving each problem.

1. I feel inadequate. I don't know how to follow up.
2. I don't click with the person I am following up. We have different personalities.
3. I don't have enough time for follow-up. I'm very busy.
4. I really don't want to follow up anyone. By nature I just don't want to do it.
5. I'm not good at making friends.

"The most significant thing I have learned in this study is:

____

____

____

____."

My Action This Week—Begin Building

Your assignment this week is to begin your ministry of teaching and training the Christian or Christians you are following up. Following the how-to's under *Let's Get Started,* set up your meeting time and begin to study the material together.

Be prepared to share your follow-up experience at your next meeting.

My Personal Study This Week

- 1 Thessalonians 2:1-12 and 2:17 through 3:13. What principles do I find in these Scripture verses that Paul used in caring for Christians and helping them grow? How can I apply these principles to my ministry?
- 1 Thessalonians 1:1-10 and 2:13-16. List all the results seen from Paul's ministry. Which results do I especially want to trust God for in my ministry?

10

Dare to Multiply

Let's suppose that you and four other friends decided to spend the next twenty years of your lives reaching the world for Christ. You got your heads together, plotted your strategy, and laid out your plan. Each of you would commit yourselves to a plan of *spiritual addition,* setting up meetings and personal appointments to share Christ with at least twenty-five people every day, for twenty years. That means that you would collectively share Christ with nearly one million people. Now that would be some kind of accomplishment.

But reaching one million people is never going to reach the world, so you decide to find a different strategy. Each year you and your four friends would select two individuals whom you would disciple, training them to feed themselves from the Word, showing them how to share their faith and how to minister to new Christians. At the end of one year each of your disciples would be ready to disciple two more Christians. There would now be fifteen of you involved in discipleship ministries—not a big crowd, but it's a start.

However, if each of you trained two more for a year, you would then have a total of forty-five, the next year 135, and the next year 405. You would have developed a *multiplication network.* In ten years there would be 295,000 in your multiplication network. In fifteen years you would have 71,744,535 and in nineteen years over five billion—more than the present population of the world!

Now, not everyone is going to become a multiplying disciple at one-year intervals. God works uniquely in everyone's life. And of course there will be dropouts. But the point is still well made. If you want to reach people with the message of Christ you will want to do it through multiplication. *It's God's idea* (Genesis 1:27; 2 Timothy 2:2).

Paul's Ministry Plan

In this study we are going to talk about how you can become a spiritual multiplier. *A multiplication ministry is really a continuation of the things you have started in follow-up.* Being a servant, a teacher, and a friend is simply carried on and intensified.

In 2 Timothy 2:2, Paul gives us a clear overview of how we can begin to be spiritual multipliers. Listen to what he says. *"And the things which you have heard me say in the presence of many witnesses, these entrust to faithful men, who will be able to teach others also"* (NASB).
If you were to break this verse down into four segments, four specific parts, what would they be?

1. ______________________________
2. ______________________________
3. ______________________________
4. ______________________________

Listening and Learning

Our ministry of multiplication really begins when we apply the first segment of 2 Timothy 2:2: *"And the things which you have heard me say."*

To be one who is giving out to others we first need to be taking in spiritual food ourselves. In other words, to be a discipler, you need to be discipled. You need to be learning from someone who is leading you.

What are some of the things Timothy was learning from Paul? Make a special note of these things.

1 Timothy 4:11-16? ____________________

____

____

____

From 2 Timothy 2:22-26? ________________________________

____

____

____

2 Timothy 4:1-5? ________________________________

____

____

____

In 2 Timothy 2:2 we have four generations of spiritual multiplication. *Paul* is the first, *Timothy* is the second, *faithful men* are the third, and *others* are the fourth. Multiplying spiritual training from one generation to another had to begin with Paul and the specific things he taught Timothy.

Are You Learning?

Who has had the greatest impact on your spiritual growth?

____

What would you consider the most significant spiritual lessons you have learned from this individual?

____

____

____

____

What are the five most important things you would teach your disciples?

1. ______________________________
2. ______________________________
3. ______________________________
4. ______________________________
5. ______________________________

Discipling in Groups

The second principle we find in 2 Timothy 2:2 is found in the statement, "*in the presence of many witnesses.*"

This may seem like the most difficult part of this verse to understand. What is Paul saying? If we look back at Paul's ministry with Timothy, we find that there were times when Paul taught and challenged Timothy in the presence of other Christians (1 Timothy 6:12; 4:14). The witnesses could have been those present.

But Paul, in this statement, is also drawing Timothy's attention to the fact that *he discipled men in groups,* a principle that we should take into consideration.

List several reasons why you think it would be wise to have a group of disciples rather than just one?

____

____

____

In your opinion, what size group would be best, and why?

____

____

____

Jesus had all the spiritual gifts and resources possible, and still he chose only twelve disciples. From those twelve he chose three with whom he spent most of his time. Why? Because the time he had would not allow him to do a quality job of building men if he worked with too many. He would be spread too thin, and his multiplication ministry would have broken down.

This is a good guideline for you. Two or three disciples is a good number with which to begin. Your ministry of evangelism must still go on, but as you train others they can help with the follow-up and discipleship.

Pass It On

The third segment of 2 Timothy 2:2 is this, "*these things* [that you have learned] *entrust to faithful men.*"
What do you think it means to *entrust* what you have learned to others? ______________________________

____

____

The dictionary tells us that entrust means *to invest a trust or a responsibility. To commit as if with trust or confidence.* In this verse Paul is not talking about just casual communication from one Christian to another. He is talking about building leaders—multipliers—people who will be entrusted with communicating the most critical message in the world, and that requires trust.

If you had the cure for cancer, and you wanted that cure communicated, whom would you *entrust* with the message? Why?

To whom does Paul instruct Timothy to entrust his message?

How would you describe a faithful person?

Give an example of someone you know who you think is faithful. Describe why this person is faithful.

Paul is not talking about men and women who are just faithful believers, but faithful in the sense of *trustworthy, true to one's word, loyal, can be relied upon, thorough.*

So when Paul is talking about entrusting faithful men, he is talking about investing his time in people who are loyal. These people will take what they have learned and pass it on to others. Paul was talking about people who were not quitters, but those who would stick with the job.

Developing Leaders

The fourth thing Paul tells Timothy is that he is to enlist faithful ones *"who will be able to teach others also."* How would you describe a person who is able to teach others?

____

____

____

Do you think that in using the word "able" Paul was talking about ability or character? ______________________

How would you describe character? What are some evidences of character? ______________________________________

____

____

____

____

When Paul tells Timothy to invest his life in *able men* he is talking about people who will someday be *able to lead*, leaders of multiplication. Now just who is an able person?

First, he is *someone who has ability, but not unique abilities.* Leading is something we can all do, whether we are leading large numbers of people or just a few. We don't have to be exceptionally gifted.

Second, he is a person who is *learning from God's Word,* in order that he can pass it on to others.

Third, an able person is one who is *growing in CHARACTER.* This is primarily what Paul is talking about when he uses the word "able." *"These things commit as a trust to trustworthy men who are of such a CHARACTER as to be adequate to teach others also."*[1]

Character includes such things as honesty, humility, faith, confidence, teachability, selflessness. Qualities like this grow as we grow spiritually. It is character that makes us adequate.

As you lead others, why do you think your character is more important than your ability? ______________________

____

____

____

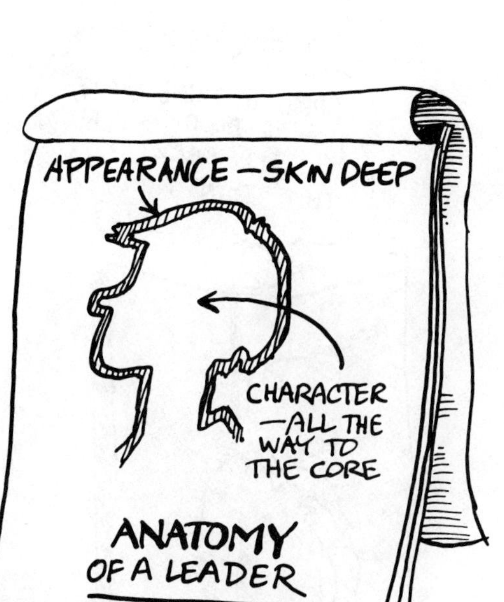

As you look for potential disciples for your multiplication group, what are some things you could look for that would indicate that he or she is *growing* in character?

How has God been building character in your life? In what areas is character necessary if we are going to lead others?

The purpose, then, of your multiplication ministry is to build up others and train them to do what you are doing. *Leadership* × *leadership* = the fulfillment of the Great Commission (Matthew 28:18-20).

Selecting Potential Multipliers

Where do we find men and women for our multiplication groups? First, we are not looking for super-Christians. We are looking for people who simply want to grow spiritually, who want to be used by God, even through they might be green in their walk with Christ. Don't disqualify yourself or someone else because of inexperience. Even if you are young, you can be a multiplier.

COME TO THINK OF IT, I WAS PRETTY GREEN MYSELF BACK AT THAT POINT!

Those you are following up will be your prime candidates. When you have completed ten to twelve weeks of study with them, many will be ready for a new challenge and commitment. Other candidates will be younger Christians in your church and campus organizations. However, not everyone grows spiritually at the same rate, so some will not be ready for this kind of challenge. It will be your job to challenge those who are indicating a desire to grow spiritually.

What, in your opinion, would be some indications that a young Christian is ready to join a multiplication group?

In the book, *So You Want to Lead Students,* I have outlined the how-to's for *whom to challenge* to your group, *how to challenge them, suggestions for materials,* and *how to lead your group.*

Putting It All Together

We have discovered that there is a difference between spiritual addition and multiplication. Explain this difference.

Which is a more effective way to reach your community, and even your world for Christ?

Why?

Have you thought about your life objective? How do you want to make your life count? Describe any objectives and goals you have for your life and the type of ministry you want to have.

"The most significant thing I have learned in this study is

."

My Action

When you have completed your follow-up you will want to begin your discipleship group. Here are some books that will help you. They can be found at your Christian bookstore.

- *So You Want to Lead Students* (Tyndale House Publishers).
- *A Guidebook to Discipleship* by Hartman & Sutherland (Eugene, OR: Harvest House Publishers, 1976).
- *The Master Plan of Evangelism* by Robert E. Coleman (Old Tappan, NJ: Fleming H. Revell Company, 1978).

Materials to study in your discipleship group include:

- *So You Want to Get into the Race.*
- *So You Want to Set the Pace.* (You can simply take others through the studies you have just completed.) Both books are available from Tyndale House Publishers, Box 80, Wheaton, IL 60187.

My Personal Study This Week

- Luke 6:12-16. What was Jesus' first priority before he chose his disciples? What principle from these verses will you apply to your ministry?
- Titus 1:6-9; 2:6-8. What are the standards for one who disciples others? In what areas do you want to see personal growth?
- 2 Timothy 2:1-13. As you think of life goals, what principles from this passage can you apply to your life?
- Over the next month read through the complete books of 1 and 2 Timothy and Titus. Record all the truths, commandments, and principles that you need to apply to your life and your ministry.

[1]*Word Studies in the Greek New Testament*, volume 2, by Kenneth S. Wuest (Grand Rapids, MI: Wm. B. Eerdmans Publishing Company).